Nahda's Family

The author and publishers are deeply grateful to the Chaudry family, without whose selfless assistance this book could not have been produced.

Published by A & C Black (Publishers) Ltd
35 Bedford Row, London WC1R 4JH

ISBN 0 7136 1732 2

First published in 1977
Reprinted 1981, 1987

Designed by Karen Bowen

Printed in Hong Kong by Dai Nippon Printing Co. Ltd

Nahda's Family

Madeleine Blakeley

Photographs by Jeremy Finlay

Adam & Charles Black · London

My name is Nahda. I'll be 12 this year. In the register at school my name is down as Nahda Chaudry, but I have another name as well – it's Tasneem: so my proper name is Nahda Tasneem Chaudry. All the girls in our family have that name – and my mum too.

My mum's name is Safia Tasneem Chaudry. She's the best mum anyone could have. Once, at school, we had to write a composition about 'My Hero', and I couldn't really think of anyone to write about. All the others were doing people like Donny Osmond and Kevin Keegan, but then I thought about the bad headaches my mum gets when all the family make a noise, and I thought about how she cooks good dinners for us all, and how she explains things to us, and answers our questions and tells us stories, and really loves us. I think my teacher thought I was a bit funny writing about my mum.

Then there's my sister Shahda, who's ten, and my little sister Farah, who's only three. My sisters and my little brothers call me *baji*. That's an Urdu word which means 'big sister'. The girls who go to the mosque call me *baji* too. I'm the monitor in charge of the girls at our mosque. That means that I have to look after them when our teacher isn't there, and I have to make sure that they are practising reading their Holy Koran properly.

We all go to the mosque every day after school for about two hours – except Farah because she is still too small. My little brothers, Amjid and Amer, come too. They wear their *topi*, which are small hats. All Muslim men wear a hat when they read the Holy Koran and when they pray to God. We girls wear our *burka*, which covers our head and arms.

مدرسة تعليم الدين
MADRESSA TALEEM-UL-DEEN

My dad is called Atta Mohammed Chaudry. He works in a mill (like a factory) now, but he used to be a bus driver. He's very clever – he's always reading and talking about things from history. Perhaps you know something about the history of Muslim people already.

My dad seems to know everything about our religion and our history. He knows about Christians and Jewish people too, and he has been to Jerusalem and to Mecca: he has seen the Kaba, and the beautiful buildings of the Middle East. Sometimes when he talks about Mohammed, our great prophet, or about Pakistan or Saudi Arabia, I wish I could learn all he knows. I don't understand everything he tells us, but I suppose if I read and study I'll be able to one day.

I go to school of course. I started at the secondary school last year. I'm not in the top band – mainly because my English isn't really good enough yet. I think one of the reasons is that when I was six, till when I was eight, all my family went to Pakistan, and of course while I was there I spoke Urdu or Punjabi.

When we came back to England I had to try and catch up with all the English I had forgotten. I was lucky because at least in my school there was a teacher who used to help me a lot – but still I suppose I haven't caught up properly yet. I can speak Urdu and Punjabi, and my mum is going to teach me to read and write Urdu when I stop going to the mosque – that'll be quite soon. I can read Arabic of course, because I have read all the Holy Koran. And now I'm trying to learn French at school.

Shahda and Amer go to the Junior school where I used to go. And Amjid's in the Infants. Farah goes to her 'school' too – that's what she calls a playgroup at the Children's Centre where my mum goes every Wednesday afternoon. Mum likes going there because it gets her out of the house, and she talks to other Pakistani and Indian women, and helps the ones who can't speak English very well.

My mum speaks English very well. She learnt it at school in Pakistan – but she wants to practise writing it properly too. While she's having her lesson, Farah has a marvellous time playing with other little children. They've got lots of toys at the Children's Centre – just like a little nursery school.

My mum's just started shift work at this mill. She's a winder. She likes going to work – I think it takes her mind off things that worry her. I help quite a lot if she's out when we all come home from school, and so does my dad. Going to work means that she gets a break from being in our little house.

It *is* a little house – but we have a back yard to play in. And a marvellous big attic room where we all go and read or bang about sometimes to be out of our mum's way.

Downstairs we stay mainly in the back room – the front room is usually kept fairly clean for when there are visitors. The front room isn't such a nice room as the back – not so friendly and comfortable. We have a big cellar too, where we store things, and two bedrooms and a big green bathroom.

My mum does all the cooking in the back room. If she was in Pakistan she'd cook on a fire in the open air. It's easier on a gas cooker! She makes us wonderful meals. I stay at school for dinners, and we have a choice of meals. I usually have eggs or fish instead of meat, because Muslim people only eat the meat of animals which have been killed in a ritual way. We get our meat from Muslim butchers, but I suppose schools can't really do that. Of course we never eat pork. My Indian friends at school sometimes eat the meat dishes, but if it's beef they have the fish or eggs like me, because most Indians don't eat beef.

I remember quite a lot about Pakistan because I lived there for two years. Our family comes from a region called Bahawulpur. My mum's family has a farm there, and so has my dad's. They grow beautiful mangoes, oranges and lemons, and all kinds of vegetables and crops. When we went to Pakistan I remember feeling that I could run about where I wanted and still be safe. You didn't have to stay in a small noisy house.

In fact we really lived outside – and slept outside too when it was very hot. And of course we had all our big family nearby – there was always someone to talk to or someone to play with. My aunty always had time to comfort us if we cried, and my uncle (my mum's younger brother who is a doctor in the Pakistan army now) loved spending time with us children.

Some of our relations in England live in the south. Dad took us all there once in our car. As soon as we started off Amjid said 'Are we there yet?' It was a really long journey, and we got lost a couple of times. As you can imagine, it's quite difficult taking seven people away on holiday, but we managed it, and I liked seeing another part of the country. It's quite different from Yorkshire. The only thing that nearly spoilt the holiday for me was my cousin. When he and Amer get together they get so excited they drive us all mad!

Sometimes my mum talks to me about what it was like when she was my age at school in Pakistan. Her school was only for girls. Muslims really like boys and girls to go to separate schools, especially after they are about 11 or 12. but of course this isn't often possible in England.

My mum wore a uniform – white *shalwar* with a blue tunic and white scarf. I wear a uniform to school – grey trousers with a white blouse and grey jumper. We all usually change our clothes when we get home from school. Shahda likes wearing trousers and blouses best, but I like shalwar or long dresses. On special occasions, like when we go to the cinema, or when visitors come, I wear my new shalwar and tunic, with the new fashion of shalwar, which are wide at the ankles. My mum sews a lot of our clothes.

The best times are when relations or friends come to visit us, or at weekends when we go out somewhere in the car. Sometimes we go to Bradford to see films made in India or Pakistan, and sometimes we just go to the park, or outside the town for a little walk.

Eid is a good time too, when we visit friends and relations, and we all have new clothes to wear. On that special day, which comes at the end of the month when Muslims fast between sunrise and sunset, all the men from round our way go to the Parish Hall for a prayer meeting, and when they come home we have such a lot of food and all kinds of fruit and sweets.

That month of fasting – called Ramdan – is a difficult time. Muslims all try not to eat anything during the day. They do it for God. Of course people who are very young or very old, or sick people, or women who are expecting babies don't have to fast. When you have fasted you feel you have really done something for God – and it makes you think a bit harder about people who maybe have that feeling of emptiness in their stomachs every day!

Another happy time was when Farah was born. She was such a small perfect baby. Lots of people came to our house to see her. My mum had her at home – she didn't go to hospital. I had to look after the others and help all the time, though my aunty came in from next door and did some of the cooking. (She's not really my aunty, but that's what we call her.) I remember we had to be very quiet while my mum was resting. Now Farah's a real little girl. And she plays and copies us. When she hears music on the tape recorder she starts dancing. She can speak English a little bit too.

Our mum doesn't like us watching television much. I have homework to do, and there isn't much time when I get home from school before we go to the mosque. I seem to be busy all the time – I suppose it's because I'm the oldest. The others help a bit – even Amjid and Farah pretend to sweep the floor when I get the brush out after dinner in the evening.

I have some good friends. Our class at school is friendly – except for a few stupid children who always seem to make a row, whether the lesson is interesting or not. Some teachers seem to like us and give us good work to do, and others don't, but I expect all schools are like that.

Sometimes I think about what will happen to me when I'm older. I want to stay as free as a bird. I should like to go to college later on. My mum got married when she was still a teenager, and that meant that she couldn't finish her education. That's why she wants to do some studying now. She wants me to work hard, and get some qualifications – and the other children too of course. I wonder if I'll be able to? I know it's difficult. And I expect my ideas might change as I get older. I have talked to Indian and Pakistani girls who are older than me – and they tell me that their parents are looking for boys for them to marry. I wonder what'll happen?

It's handy having shops nearby that stay open late and at weekends. The shop on the corner sells all the kinds of things that my mum needs when she's cooking. They even get vegetables like okra (which we call *bhindi*) which are hard to find in English greengrocers. All the spices are there too; and flour for making chapattis and rice. We buy that in great big bags, which last a long time. I think it's cheaper to buy them that way.

Our next door neighbours have a shop too – they sell all sorts of things – material and clothes from Pakistan, as well as English things which everyone needs in their house. I like the ornaments and jewellery you can buy there – some of the rings and necklaces are real gold. My mum has some beautiful gold things, which she had as a present from her father and my dad when she got married.

I wonder if you know a family like ours? Maybe your family is a bit like ours, even if you live in a different sort of house in a different part of the country. What I like about my family is that we love each other and that won't change whatever happens.